W9-APS-183

MN¡

DISCARDED
From Nashville Public Library

NASHVILLE PUBLIC LIBRARY
FOUNDATION

*This book
made possible
through generous gifts
to the
Nashville Public Library
Foundation Book Fund*

NPLF.ORG

THE NEGRO Leagues

by Gregory N. Peters

CAPSTONE PRESS
a capstone imprint

Nashville Public Library

Trailblazers Books are published by Capstone Press,
1710 Roe Crest Drive, North Mankato, Minnesota 56003
www.capstonepub.com

Copyright © 2014 by Capstone Press, a Capstone imprint. All rights reserved.
No part of this publication may be reproduced in whole or in part, or stored
in a retrieval system, or transmitted in any form or by any means, electronic,
mechanical, photocopying, recording, or otherwise, without written
permission of the publisher.

Library of Congress Cataloging-in-Publication Data
Peters, Gregory N.
The Negro Leagues / by Gregory N. Peters.
pages cm. — (Trailblazers. sports and recreation)
Includes bibliographical references and index.
Summary: "Describes the history of the Negro Leagues, the only option for
African-American baseball players until the color barrier was broken in the
late 1940s"—Provided by publisher.
ISBN 978-1-4765-8015-9 (library binding)
1. Negro leagues—History—Juvenile literature. 2. Baseball—United
States—History—Juvenile literature. I. Title.
GV875.N35P48 2014
796.357'640973—dc23   2013030189

Editorial Credits
Christine Peterson, editor; Gene Bentdahl, designer; Eric Gohl, media
researcher; Eric Manske, production specialist

Photo Credits
AP Photo: Charlie Riedel, 42; Capstone: 9; Corbis: Bettmann, 18, 22, 25, 27,
33, 37 (top), 38, epa/John G. Mabanglo, 37 (bottom); Getty Images: Time Life
Pictures/George Strock, 20, Transcendental Graphics/Mark Rucker, cover,
4, 7, 10, 14, 28–29, 40–41; Newscom: Icon SMI/TSN, 30, 34, Picture History,
12–13, 17

Printed in China by Nordica.
1013/CA21301911
029013   007739NORDS14

TABLE OF CONTENTS

Hall of Famers Satchel Paige, left, and Josh Gibson

plaque – a flat, decorated piece of metal or wood hung on a wall

Major League – the two main baseball groups in the United States—the American League and the National League

CHAPTER 1

Unknown Legend

What comes to mind when you hear the words "Baseball Hall of Fame"? Do you think about pitchers who can throw blazing fastballs? Do you imagine hitters who can smash a ball over a distant fence? The best of the best are honored in the National Baseball Hall of Fame and Museum.

There are 300 baseball legends in the Hall. **Plaques** are hung to honor them. One bronze plaque stands out. It honors Josh Gibson. The bronze writing reads "power-hitting catcher who hit almost 800 home runs." That's an amazing number.

"I played with Willie Mays and against Hank Aaron," said Hall of Famer Monte Irvin. "They were tremendous players, but they were no Josh Gibson. You saw him hit, and you took your hat off."

Have you ever heard of Gibson? He played baseball in the Negro Leagues. Gibson led the Homestead Grays to nine straight championships. He played in nine East-West All-Star games. His 84 home runs in 1936 are still talked about today. But Josh Gibson never played **Major League** Baseball. He never got the chance.

Whites-Only Baseball

Slavery officially ended in 1865 after the Civil War (1861–1865). African-Americans were free. By the late 1800s, whites and African-Americans played on the same baseball teams. Some states such as Ohio had **integrated** teams in which players of different races competed together. But the players were not always treated equally. Moses Fleetwood "Fleet" Walker was one of the few African-American players in the league. He was a catcher. He played for the Toledo Blue Stockings. Many people did not like Walker playing with white players. Newspapers wrote **racist**  things about him. People screamed mean words against African-Americans from the stands. Walker could not eat meals with his teammates on trips.

In 1883 the Blue Stockings played the Chicago White Stockings. Chicago's star player refused to play. He would not share the field with an African-American. Many events like this happened. Some white players wanted **segregated** teams with no black players allowed.

Fleet Walker (back row, far right) joined the Syracuse Stars in 1888.

integrated – accepting of all races

racist – believing that one race is better than another race

segregated – separated by race

In 1890 white team owners and executives met. They agreed to **ban** future contracts with African-American players.

Barnstorming

African-American players began to form their own teams. Hundreds of African-American teams formed throughout the United States. There were teams from Alabama to New York. One team was the Kansas City Monarchs. Another team was the Philadelphia Stars.

By the end of World War I (1914–1918), African-American baseball had become popular. The teams traveled around the country. This was called **barnstorming**. The teams played **exhibition** games that were very entertaining. There were teams such as the Tennessee Rats and the Ethiopian Clowns. These traveling teams won many games. Players liked to show off their skills. Hitters might get down on their knees, waiting for the next pitch. A hitter might run the bases backward after hitting a home run. Hundreds of people paid to watch these entertaining games.

ban - to forbid or make something illegal

barnstorm - to tour an area playing exhibition games after the regular season

exhibition - a public display of skills

Negro Leagues Teams 1930s and 1940s

Most teams in the Negro Leagues were based in the Northeast and Midwest.

Members of the All Nations barnstorming team of Kansas City in about 1915

CHAPTER 2

A New League

The years following the 1890 ban were hard for African-Americans. There were still some laws that prevented them from being truly free. The **Jim Crow laws** led to segregation. These laws separated African-Americans and whites in hospitals, schools, and even sports. There were hard feelings between many African-Americans and whites.

African-Americans were not allowed to play baseball with white players. So African-Americans built their own baseball world. In the beginning baseball teams barnstormed across the country. They played any **opponent** they could find. Barnstorming also allowed them to connect to the fans. Traveling teams paraded through the cities.

In 1920 the Negro National League was formed in Kansas City, Missouri. There were eight teams and many great players in the league. Months later a Negro Southern League formed in Atlanta, Georgia. Both leagues enjoyed great success.

Jim Crow laws – laws that enforced racial segregation

opponent – a person who competes against another person

On the Road

In many ways the Negro Leagues were just like the major leagues. They had their own teams, uniforms, and stadiums. By 1924 there was even a Negro **World Series**. That year the Kansas City Monarchs won the nine-game series against Hilldale of Philadelphia. The Monarchs had two great pitchers. They were Wilber "Bullet" Rogan and José Méndez. The star player for Hilldale was William Julius "Judy" Johnson. All three stars eventually were named to the Hall of Fame.

The champion Kansas City Monarchs

Players in the Negro Leagues and the major leagues were paid around the same amount. They made between $150 and $400 each month. They were given money for food. But many Negro Leagues players experienced hard times. Some owners could not pay them on time. Some players did not get paid at all.

World Series - the professional championship games at the end of the baseball season

Smokey Joe Williams

Players in the Negro Leagues had to travel a lot. On the road they experienced segregation. Many hotels would not accept African-American players as guests. Sometimes the players would have to sleep in the dugout at the baseball stadium.

Many Negro Leagues teams did not have extra players. This meant all the team members had to play. Most major league pitchers played only when they pitched. They played only once or twice a week. But pitchers in the Negro Leagues had to play almost every game. If a pitcher got hurt, then an outfielder with a strong arm pitched.

The life of a Negro Leagues player was not full of **luxuries**. The players traveled by bus. They played a game and then got back on the bus to go to the next game.

The Negro Leagues made it through good times and bad times. There were great players such as Oscar Charleston, Satchel Paige, and Smokey Joe Williams. The players entertained fans in city after city. Williams **impressed** fans with his amazing fastballs. One opponent said Williams' pitches seemed as if they were coming "off a mountain top."

---

luxury - something that is not needed but adds great ease and comfort
impress - to make someone think highly of you

Greenlee's Team

For years the Negro Leagues experienced difficulties. But they finally became successful in 1932. That's when Gus Greenlee bought the Pittsburgh Crawfords.

Greenlee was a smart man. He knew how to make money. He owned the Crawford Bar and Grille in Pittsburgh. It was a restaurant and dance hall. **Jazz** stars such as Duke Ellington and Count Basie performed there.

The Homestead Grays were the most important Negro Leagues team in Pittsburgh. Greenlee wanted to create a Pittsburgh team better than the Grays. He wanted to create a Pittsburgh **rivalry**.

Greenlee started to get great players like Satchel Paige, Josh Gibson, and James Thomas "Cool Papa" Bell. The Crawfords soon became the most powerful team in the league.

The 1932 Pittsburgh Crawfords

jazz – a style of music in which players often make up
their own tunes and add notes in unexpected places

rivalry – a fierce feeling of competition

Alec Radcliffe (right), who spent most of his career with the Chicago American Giants, appeared in 11 East-West All-Star Games. He watches a 1942 game with Art Pennington (left) and Herman Andrews.

All-Stars!

The major league had its first **All-Star Game** in 1933. Greenlee thought the Negro Leagues should have its own all-star game. He organized the East-West All-Star Game. It was his biggest **accomplishment**.

This game became the most important African-American sporting event. The best players showed off their talents in Chicago's Comiskey Park. Players from the Homestead Grays, the Pittsburgh Crawfords, and the Kansas City Monarchs played. So did players from the Cleveland Buckeyes, the Chicago American Giants, and the Newark Eagles. They played for huge audiences.

Players were chosen through fan voting in African-American newspapers. Fans traveled to the game from all over the country. They wanted to witness the amazing batting power and thundering pitches of the Negro Leagues All-Stars.

Sam Lacy, a writer for the Baltimore *Afro-American* newspaper, enjoyed attending the event. "It was a holiday for at least 48 hours," he said. "People would just about come from everywhere, mainly because it was such a **spectacle**." The players and fans showed that the Negro Leagues were impressive and popular.

All-Star Game - an exhibition game played by the best players in the leagues

accomplishment - something that has been done successfully

spectacle - a public show or display, especially on a large scale

Satchel Paige had a famous high kick.

CHAPTER 3

Baseball Heroes

Some of the players of the Negro Leagues were the greatest of all time.

Satchel Paige

Leroy "Satchel" Paige was an exciting player. Before each pitch he would wind up his arm like a windmill. Paige had a number of special pitches. They were called the Midnight Creeper, the Four-Day Rider, and the Bat Dodger. Another was called the Hurry-up Ball. Each pitch had its unique speed and movement. Some seemed to dance in the air. "He threw *fire*," Buck Leonard said. Leonard claimed he never got a hit off Paige in 17 years. That might have been an exaggeration. Truth is, Satchel Paige was one of the most amazing pitchers who ever lived.

Buck Leonard

Walter Fenner "Buck" Leonard may not have gotten hits off Paige, but he was a great hitter. Leonard's father died when he was a kid. At 16 he worked for the railroad. He worked during the day. He played baseball in the afternoon.

In a close call at home plate, Ted "Double Duty" Radcliffe of the West tags out the East's Josh Gibson. It happened during the 1944 East-West All-Star Game.

Buck Leonard was a smooth-fielding first baseman. He had a swift, powerful swing. The Homestead Grays built their great team around Leonard. He was called "the Lou Gehrig of the Negro Leagues."

Josh Gibson

Josh Gibson was called the "black Babe Ruth." Gibson **awed** fans with his long home runs. The ball seemed to explode off his bat like a rocket. He used to say, "A homer a day will boost my pay."

Gibson died of a stroke at age 35. He left a great **legacy**. Gibson hit almost 800 home runs. He played in the East-West All-Star Game nine times. He won the batting title four times. Satchel Paige said Gibson was "the greatest hitter who ever lived."

awe - to fill with great wonder, fear, or respect

legacy - qualities and actions that one is remembered for; something that is passed on to future generations

23

Cool Papa Bell

James Thomas "Cool Papa" Bell was built for speed. People said he was the fastest player in the Negro Leagues. Bell was born in Mississippi.

In 1920 Bell left the South and moved to St. Louis, Missouri. He went to play in the Negro Leagues. He started out as a pitcher. He was nicknamed "Cool Papa" because he was very calm. Bell was an excellent hitter and fielder. In the outfield he showed his speed. How fast was he? Gibson said that Bell was so fast that when he turned out the light at night, he was in bed before the room got dark!

Bell was **inducted** into the National Baseball Hall of Fame in 1974. He was one of the first players from the Negro Leagues to be named to the Hall of Fame.

induct - to formally admit someone into a position or place of honor

Cool Papa Bell (seated, left) was inducted into the Hall of Fame with (from left) Mickey Mantle, Joco Conlan, and Whitey Ford.

Home Run Brown

Willard "Home Run" Brown played for the Kansas City Monarchs. Satchel Paige was his teammate. Brown was a powerful player. He was so good that he **terrorized** pitchers. Brown played in eight East-West All-Star Games.

Brown played winter baseball in **Latin America**. He was a hero in Puerto Rico. He won three batting titles. They called him *Ese Hombre,* which is Spanish for "That Man." Brown came back to play for the Kansas City Monarchs.

Some say he was a better player than Josh Gibson. It was Gibson who gave him the nickname "Home Run." Brown played in the major leagues for a short time. He was the first African-American to hit a home run in the American League.

terrorize - to fill or overcome with fear

Latin America - the part of the American continents south of the United States

Negro Leaguers Willard Brown (right) and Hank Thompson (left) signed with the St. Louis Browns of the American League in 1947. They sat in the dugout with their manager, Muddy Ruel.

Mule Suttles

George "Mule" Suttles was another power hitter of the Negro Leagues. He got his nickname because people said he was as strong as a mule. Suttles played on many teams. He became popular as a Chicago American Giant. He played in five East-West All-Star Games at Comiskey Park.

Suttles smashed many home runs into the seats.

Mule Suttles (back row, middle) was a player and manager with the Newark Eagles.

Over the years Suttles became a **mentor**. He gave younger players **advice**. Clarence Israel of the Newark Eagles said, "He was considered my dad. Suttles was the most gentle person I ever saw."

mentor - a wise and faithful adviser or teacher

advice - suggestions about what to do about a problem

Jackie Robinson played shortstop for the Kansas City Monarchs for one season.

CHAPTER 4

Changing Times

African-Americans fought and died in World War II (1939–1945). At the same time, they were still barred from Major League Baseball. The general manager of the Brooklyn Dodgers wanted to get rid of the Jim Crow laws.

The general manager's name was Branch Rickey. He had a plan to bring African-American players to his team. Rickey was a kind person. However, he had other **motives** for integration. He wanted a better team. In 1945 Rickey wrote, "My only purpose is to be fair to all people and my selfish objective is to win baseball games."

Rickey was looking for a special player. He needed someone who was talented, confident, and patient. The player had to be brave. He would have to stand up to **discrimination**. Rickey found all of these qualities in a star player named Jackie Robinson. Robinson played for the Kansas City Monarchs.

motive - a reason why a person does something

discrimination - treating people unfairly because of their skin color or class

Courage and Talent

Jack Roosevelt Robinson was born in Georgia. His mother raised him. In 1920 the family moved to California. Robinson was a great athlete in high school and in college. He became the first student at the University of California, Los Angeles (UCLA), to win **varsity** letters in four sports. They were baseball, basketball, football, and track. He also **excelled** in swimming and tennis.

Athletic talent ran in the Robinson family. Jackie's older brother Matthew competed in the 1936 **Olympics**. He won a silver medal. But when Matthew returned to California, he could only get a job sweeping city streets. Jackie would never forget this.

In 1942 Jackie Robinson was **drafted** into the U.S. Army. He served as a second lieutenant. One day Robinson had to ride the bus during training. The driver told him to move to the back of the bus. That was where African-Americans were supposed to ride by law. Robinson refused. He thought it was wrong and unfair. He was arrested and put on trial in a military court. Robinson was later found not guilty. Soon he would need to draw on his courage again.

---

varsity – any first-string team

excel – to do extremely well

Olympics – an international sporting contest held every four years

draft – the process of choosing a person to serve in the military or join a sports team

Jackie Robinson was a star football player at UCLA.

Jackie Robinson, with Branch Rickey, signs a contract
to play with the Brooklyn Dodgers.

Crossing the "Color Line"

Branch Rickey met with Robinson in August 1945. At first he told Robinson he was looking for players to start a new African-American team. The team would be called the Brown Dodgers. Then Rickey told Robinson the truth. He wanted him to play for the Brooklyn Dodgers. He wanted Robinson to change the look of baseball in the United States. "I want you to be the first Negro player in the Major League. I've been trying to give you some idea of the punishment you will have to absorb. Can you take it?" Rickey asked.

Rickey described situations Robinson might face. In these situations racist people took their anger out on Robinson. Rickey wanted to know how Robinson would react. Robinson kept calm. He would be the man to break the "color line."

Robinson signed the contract on October 23, 1945. He was given a Dodgers uniform, number 42.

Robinson didn't play his first major league game until April 1946. A lot of people were hoping he would never play. Robinson and his family received death threats. Almost all the other Brooklyn Dodgers did not want him on the team. They signed a **petition**. They said they would not get on the field with an African-American man.

"I'm not signing that," Harold "Pee Wee" Reese said about the petition. "No way." Reese was the team captain. Reese stood up for Robinson many times. The other Dodgers agreed to play with Robinson, even if they were unhappy. But players on other teams acted out their hateful feelings. They hit, **taunted**, and even spat on Robinson. Angry crowds called him racist names.

Not only did Robinson **endure** these challenges, he succeeded. He won the Rookie of the Year and Most Valuable Player awards. He helped the Dodgers win six National League championships. He helped beat the New York Yankees in the 1955 World Series.

Robinson used his influence to speak out about **civil rights** for African-American athletes. He talked about discrimination before Congress. Today people honor his achievements. On Jackie Robinson Day, all Major League players wear the number 42 to pay tribute to the baseball legend. Jackie Robinson Day is held April 15 of each year.

Pee Wee Reese and Jackie Robinson practiced their double-play technique during spring training in 1950. Many years later a young fan shows his appreciation.

petition - a letter signed by many people asking leaders for a change

taunt - to use words to try to make someone angry

endure - to last for a long time

civil rights - freedoms that every person should have

Roy Campanella easily tags a runner during the 1951 All-Star Game. He had a successful 10-year career in the major leagues. He was inducted into the Hall of Fame in 1969.

CHAPTER 5

Breaking Down Barriers

After Robinson broke the color **barrier**, other Negro Leagues stars joined the major leagues. Players such as Roy Campanella and Hank Aaron left the Negro Leagues. Joe Black, Don Newcombe, and Larry Doby also left the leagues. The most talented players were gone. The Negro Leagues began to disappear.

Losing the Negro Leagues hurt many African-Americans. The leagues symbolized African-American pride.

barrier - something that prevents progress

The Negro National League shut down in 1948.
The Negro American League became smaller and
smaller over the next 10 years. The last East-West
All-Star Game was played in 1961.

The Negro Leagues had been about more
than just a game. They were deeply connected to
African-American life. Barnstorming started in the
spring. The baseball season ended in autumn. Many
African-American families headed to a ball game.

Buck O'Neil (front row, center) was a player and manager with the Kansas City Monarchs. He joined the Chicago Cubs as a scout and in 1962 became the first black coach in major league history.

But things change. More and more major league teams hired African-American players. The fans of these players often traveled far to watch them play. African-American fans wanted to watch integrated baseball. But they had to sit in segregated seats. Breaking the color line was a huge step toward freedom. But African-Americans still had a long way to go before they would be truly free and equal.

National Baseball Hall of Fame

Many of the Negro Leagues' greatest players are in the National Baseball Hall of Fame in Cooperstown, New York. Their plaques tell mostly about their baseball accomplishments. But most of these players overcame discrimination to achieve greatness.

Satchel Paige's statue at the Negro Leagues Baseball Museum in Kansas City, Missouri

Satchel Paige was inducted into the Hall of Fame in 1971. He was the first African-American pitcher in the Hall. Paige played in the major leagues. He was a 42-year-old rookie pitcher for the Cleveland Indians. Paige gave a speech when he was voted into the Hall. He talked about the talent that shined in the Negro Leagues. "There were many Satchels, there were many Joshes," he said. It was a nice tribute to all the great and brave men who played the game they loved.

The players are also remembered at the Negro Leagues Baseball Museum. It is located near downtown Kansas City.

Negro Leaguers in the National Baseball Hall of Fame

Player/Executive		Inducted	Player/Executive		Inducted
Cool Papa Bell	1903–1991	1974	*Effa Manley	1897–1981	2006
Ray Brown	1908–1965	2006	José Méndez	1887–1928	2006
Willard Brown	1915–1996	2006	Satchel Paige	1906–1982	1971
Oscar Charleston	1896–1954	1976	Alex Pompez	1890–1974	2006
Andy Cooper	1898–1941	2006	Cum Posey	1890–1946	2006
Ray Dandridge	1913–1994	1987	Bullet Rogan	1889–1967	1998
Leon Day	1916–1995	1995	Louis Santop	1890–1942	2006
Martin Dihigo	1905–1971	1977	Hilton Smith	1907–1983	2001
Rube Foster	1879–1930	1981	Turkey Stearnes	1901–1979	2000
Willie Foster	1904–1978	1996	George Suttles	1900–1966	2006
Josh Gibson	1911–1947	1972	Ben Taylor	1888–1953	2006
Frank Grant	1865–1937	2006	Cristóbal Torriente	1893–1938	2006
Pete Hill	1882–1951	2006	Willie Wells	1908–1989	1997
Monte Irvin	1919–	1973	Sol White	1868–1955	2006
Judy Johnson	1900–1989	1975	J.L.Wilkinson	1874–1964	2006
Buck Leonard	1907–1997	1972	Smokey Joe Williams	1886–1946	1999
Pop Lloyd	1884–1964	1977	Jud Wilson	1894–1963	2006
Biz Mackey	1897–1965	2006			

* First woman inducted into the National Baseball Hall of Fame

Source: National Baseball Hall of Fame and Museum and Negro Leagues Hall of Fame Members

Read More

Burgan, Michael. *The Negro Leagues.* We the People. Minneapolis: Compass Point Books, 2008.

Fishman, Cathy. *When Jackie and Hank Met.* New York: Marshall Cavendish Children, 2012.

Nelson, Kadir. *We Are the Ship: The Story of Negro League Baseball.* New York: Jump at the Sun/Hyperion Books for Children, 2008.

Price, Sean. *Jackie Robinson: Breaking the Color Barrier.* American History Through Primary Sources. Chicago: Raintree/Fusion, 2009.

Bibliography

page 5 • from *Gibson the best home run hitter in the Negro Leagues* by Tom Singer. MLB.com (http://mlb.mlb.com/mlb/history/mlb_negro_leagues_profile.jsp?player=gibson_josh)

page 15 • from *Invisible Men: Life in Baseball's Negro Leagues* by Donn Rogosin. Lincoln: University of Nebraska Press, 2007, p. 13.

page 19 • from *Black Baseball's National Showcase: The East-West All-Star Game, 1933-1953* by Larry Lester. Lincoln: University of Nebraska Press, 2001, page 3.

page 21 • from *Maybe I'll Pitch Forever: A Great Baseball Player Tells the Hilarious Story Behind the Legend* by Leroy (Satchel) Paige, as told to David Lipman. Lincoln: University of Nebraska Press, 1993, p. vi.

page 23 • from *Josh Gibson: The Power and the Darkness* by Mark Ribowsky. Urbana: University of Illinois Press, 2004, page 60.

page 23 • from *No joshing about Gibson's talents* by Larry Schwartz. ESPN.com (http://espn.go.com/sportscentury/features/00016050.html)

page 24 • from *Baseball Almanac* (http://www.baseball-almanac.com/quotes/quobell.shtml)

page 29 • from *Baseball's Ultimate Power: Ranking the All-Time Greatest Distance Home Run Hitters* by Bill Jenkinson. Guilford, Conn.: Lyons Press, 2010, page 75.

pages 31 and 35 • from *Baseball: A History of America's Game* by Benjamin G. Rader. Urbana: University of Illinois Press, 2008, pages 165, 156.

page 36 • from *Standing Beside Jackie Robinson, Reese Helped Change Baseball* by Ira Berkow. *The New York Times*, March 31, 1997. (http://www.nytimes.com/specials/baseball/bbo-reese-robinson.html)

page 42 • from *Maybe I'll Pitch Forever: A Great Baseball Player Tells the Hilarious Story Behind the Legend*, page vii.

Internet Sites

FactHound offers a safe, fun way to find Internet sites related to this book. All of the sites on FactHound have been researched by our staff.

Here's all you do:
Visit *www.facthound.com*
Type in this code: 9781476580159

Super-cool stuff!

Check out projects, games and lots more at
www.capstonekids.com

Titles in This Set

The Best of College Basketball

Muhammad Ali Boxing Legend

The Negro Leagues

Serena and Venus Williams Tennis Stars

Glossary

accomplishment (uh-KOM-plish-muhnt) • something that has been done successfully

advice (ad-VICE) • suggestions about what to do about a problem

All-Star Game (AWL-star GAME) • an exhibition game played by the best players in the leagues

awe (AW) • to fill with great wonder, fear, or respect

ban (BAN) • to forbid or make something illegal

barnstorm (BAHRN-stawrm) • to tour an area playing exhibition games after the regular season

barrier (BAR-ee-uhr) • something that prevents progress

civil rights (si-vil RYTS) • freedoms that every person should have

discrimination (dih-skrim-uh-NEY-shuhn) • treating people unfairly because of their skin color or class

draft (DRAHFT) • the process of choosing a person to serve in the military or join a sports team

endure (en-DUR) • to last for a long time

excel (ex-SEL) • to do extremely well

exhibition (ek-suh-BI-shuhn) • a public display of skills

impress (im-PRESS) • to make someone think highly of you

induct (in-DUHKT) • to formally admit someone into a position or place of honor

integrated (IN-tuh-gray-tid) • accepting of all races

jazz (JAZ) • a style of music in which players often make up their own tunes and add notes in unexpected places

Jim Crow laws (JIM KROH LAWZ) • laws that enforced racial segregation

Latin America (LAH-tin ah-MAYR-ica) • the part of the American continents south of the United States

legacy (LEG-uh-see) • qualities and actions that one is remembered for; something that is passed on to future generations

luxury (LUHG-zhuh-ree) • something that is not needed but adds great ease and comfort

major league (MAY-jur LEEG) • the two main baseball groups in the United States—the American League and the National League

mentor (MEN-tur) • a wise and faithful adviser or teacher

motive (MOH-tiv) • a reason why a person does something

Olympics (oh-LIM-piks) • an international sporting contest held every four years

opponent (uh-POH-nuhnt) • a person who competes against another person

petition (puh-TISH-uhn) • a letter signed by many people asking leaders for a change

plaque (PLAK) • a flat, decorated piece of metal or wood hung on a wall

racist (RAY-sist) • believing that one race is better than another race

rivalry (RYE-val-ree) • a fierce feeling of competition

segregated (SEG-ruh-gay-ted) • separated by race

spectacle (SPEK-tuh-kuhl) • a public show or display, especially on a large scale

taunt (TAWNT) • to use words to make someone angry

terrorize (TER-uh-rahyz) • to fill or overcome with fear

varsity (VAHR-si-tee) • any first-string team

World Series (WURLD SIHR-eez) • the professional championship games at the end of the baseball season

Index